50 Athlete Cookbook Recipes for Home

By: Kelly Johnson

Table of Contents

- Grilled Chicken Breast with Lemon and Herbs
- Quinoa Salad with Avocado and Black Beans
- Baked Salmon with Dill and Garlic
- Protein Pancakes with Berries
- Turkey Chili with Beans
- Greek Yogurt Parfait with Granola and Honey
- Veggie Stir-Fry with Tofu
- Lean Beef Tacos with Salsa and Guacamole
- Whole Wheat Pasta with Chicken and Pesto
- Egg White Omelette with Spinach and Feta
- Grilled Shrimp Skewers with Cajun Seasoning
- Sweet Potato Hash with Turkey Sausage
- Brown Rice Bowl with Grilled Vegetables
- Spinach and Berry Smoothie with Protein Powder
- Lentil Soup with Kale and Carrots
- Baked Cod with Lemon and Garlic
- Quinoa Stuffed Bell Peppers
- Oatmeal with Almond Butter and Banana
- Chicken and Vegetable Kabobs
- Greek Salad with Grilled Chicken
- Turkey Meatballs with Marinara Sauce
- Whole Wheat Wrap with Turkey, Hummus, and Veggies
- Cottage Cheese and Fruit Bowl
- Tuna Salad with Avocado and Spinach
- Black Bean and Corn Quesadillas
- Baked Sweet Potato Fries
- Chicken and Vegetable Stir-Fry with Brown Rice
- Grilled Steak with Chimichurri Sauce
- Veggie Frittata with Goat Cheese
- Quinoa and Black Bean Salad
- Greek Yogurt Chicken Salad
- Spaghetti Squash with Turkey Bolognese
- Protein Smoothie Bowl with Berries and Almond Milk
- Teriyaki Salmon with Stir-Fried Vegetables
- Turkey and Veggie Lettuce Wraps

- Whole Wheat Pasta Primavera
- Greek Yogurt Parfait with Mixed Nuts and Honey
- Lentil and Vegetable Curry
- Baked Chicken Thighs with Rosemary and Garlic
- Egg White Breakfast Burrito with Salsa
- Stuffed Portobello Mushrooms with Quinoa and Spinach
- Turkey and Black Bean Chili
- Grilled Vegetable Salad with Chickpeas
- Tofu and Vegetable Stir-Fry with Brown Rice
- Baked Cod with Mango Salsa
- Turkey and Quinoa Stuffed Zucchini
- Greek Yogurt Ranch Dip with Veggies
- Chicken Caesar Salad with Whole Wheat Croutons
- Black Bean and Sweet Potato Enchiladas
- Protein-Packed Green Smoothie with Kale and Pineapple

Grilled Chicken Breast with Lemon and Herbs

Ingredients:

- 4 boneless, skinless chicken breasts
- 2 lemons
- 2 cloves garlic, minced
- 2 tablespoons olive oil
- 1 tablespoon fresh parsley, chopped
- 1 tablespoon fresh thyme leaves
- Salt and pepper to taste

Instructions:

Preheat your grill to medium-high heat.
In a small bowl, combine the juice of one lemon, minced garlic, olive oil, chopped parsley, and thyme leaves. Season with salt and pepper to taste.
Place the chicken breasts in a shallow dish or resealable plastic bag. Pour the marinade over the chicken, making sure each piece is well coated. Marinate in the refrigerator for at least 30 minutes, or up to 4 hours for maximum flavor.
Remove the chicken from the marinade and discard any excess marinade.
Grill the chicken breasts for 6-8 minutes per side, or until they are cooked through and no longer pink in the center. The internal temperature should reach 165°F (75°C).
While the chicken is grilling, slice the remaining lemon into wedges.
Once the chicken is cooked, remove it from the grill and let it rest for a few minutes before serving.
Serve the grilled chicken breasts with lemon wedges on the side for squeezing over the top. Garnish with additional fresh herbs if desired.
Enjoy your Grilled Chicken Breast with Lemon and Herbs!

This dish pairs well with a variety of sides, such as grilled vegetables, rice, or a fresh salad.

Quinoa Salad with Avocado and Black Beans

Ingredients:

- 1 cup quinoa, rinsed
- 2 cups water or vegetable broth
- 1 can (15 ounces) black beans, drained and rinsed
- 1 ripe avocado, diced
- 1 red bell pepper, diced
- 1/2 cup cherry tomatoes, halved
- 1/4 cup red onion, finely chopped
- 1/4 cup fresh cilantro, chopped
- Juice of 1 lime
- 2 tablespoons olive oil
- 1 teaspoon ground cumin
- Salt and pepper to taste

Instructions:

In a medium saucepan, bring the water or vegetable broth to a boil. Add the quinoa and reduce the heat to low. Cover and simmer for about 15 minutes, or until the quinoa is cooked and the liquid is absorbed. Remove from heat and let it cool.

In a large mixing bowl, combine the cooked quinoa, black beans, diced avocado, diced red bell pepper, cherry tomatoes, chopped red onion, and chopped cilantro.

In a small bowl, whisk together the lime juice, olive oil, ground cumin, salt, and pepper to make the dressing.

Pour the dressing over the quinoa salad mixture and toss gently to coat all the ingredients evenly.

Taste and adjust seasoning if needed.

Chill the salad in the refrigerator for at least 30 minutes before serving to allow the flavors to meld together.

Serve chilled as a side dish or a light meal.

Enjoy your Quinoa Salad with Avocado and Black Beans!

This salad is not only nutritious and filling but also packed with flavor and texture. It's perfect for meal prep or as a side dish for picnics, potlucks, or barbecues.

Baked Salmon with Dill and Garlic

Ingredients:

- 4 salmon fillets (about 6 ounces each), skin-on or skinless
- 2 tablespoons olive oil
- 2 cloves garlic, minced
- 2 tablespoons fresh dill, chopped
- 1 tablespoon lemon juice
- Salt and pepper to taste
- Lemon slices for garnish (optional)

Instructions:

Preheat your oven to 375°F (190°C). Line a baking sheet with parchment paper or lightly grease it with oil to prevent sticking.
Place the salmon fillets on the prepared baking sheet, skin-side down if they have skin.
In a small bowl, combine the olive oil, minced garlic, chopped dill, lemon juice, salt, and pepper. Stir well to mix.
Brush or spoon the garlic-dill mixture evenly over the salmon fillets, coating them on all sides.
If desired, place a few slices of lemon on top of each fillet for extra flavor.
Bake the salmon in the preheated oven for 12-15 minutes, or until the salmon flakes easily with a fork and is cooked to your desired doneness.
Remove the salmon from the oven and let it rest for a few minutes before serving.
Serve the baked salmon hot, garnished with additional fresh dill and lemon slices if desired.
Enjoy your Baked Salmon with Dill and Garlic!

This dish pairs well with a variety of sides such as roasted vegetables, steamed greens, quinoa, or a fresh salad. It's a healthy and delicious option for any day of the week!

Protein Pancakes with Berries

Ingredients:

- 1 cup rolled oats
- 1 ripe banana
- 2 eggs
- 1 scoop (about 30g) vanilla protein powder
- 1/2 cup milk (dairy or plant-based)
- 1 teaspoon baking powder
- 1/2 teaspoon vanilla extract
- Pinch of salt
- Cooking spray or butter for greasing the pan
- Fresh berries (such as strawberries, blueberries, raspberries) for topping
- Maple syrup or honey for drizzling (optional)

Instructions:

In a blender or food processor, combine the rolled oats, banana, eggs, protein powder, milk, baking powder, vanilla extract, and salt. Blend until smooth and well combined. If the batter is too thick, you can add a little more milk to reach your desired consistency.

Heat a non-stick skillet or griddle over medium heat. Lightly grease the surface with cooking spray or butter.

Pour about 1/4 cup of batter onto the skillet for each pancake, spreading it slightly with the back of a spoon to form a circle.

Cook the pancakes for 2-3 minutes, or until bubbles start to form on the surface and the edges look set.

Carefully flip the pancakes with a spatula and cook for another 1-2 minutes on the other side, or until golden brown and cooked through.

Transfer the cooked pancakes to a plate and keep them warm while you cook the remaining batter, greasing the skillet as needed between batches.

Once all the pancakes are cooked, stack them on plates and top with fresh berries.

Drizzle with maple syrup or honey if desired, and serve immediately.

Enjoy your Protein Pancakes with Berries!

These protein-packed pancakes are not only delicious but also a great way to start your day with a healthy and satisfying breakfast. They're perfect for fueling your body before or after a workout, or anytime you need a nutritious meal.

Turkey Chili with Beans

Ingredients:

- 1 tablespoon olive oil
- 1 onion, diced
- 3 cloves garlic, minced
- 1 red bell pepper, diced
- 1 yellow bell pepper, diced
- 1 pound ground turkey
- 2 tablespoons chili powder
- 1 teaspoon ground cumin
- 1 teaspoon paprika
- 1/2 teaspoon dried oregano
- 1/4 teaspoon cayenne pepper (optional, for added heat)
- Salt and pepper to taste
- 1 can (15 ounces) diced tomatoes
- 1 can (15 ounces) tomato sauce
- 1 can (15 ounces) kidney beans, drained and rinsed
- 1 can (15 ounces) black beans, drained and rinsed
- 1 cup chicken broth
- Optional toppings: shredded cheese, diced avocado, chopped cilantro, sour cream, lime wedges, tortilla chips

Instructions:

Heat the olive oil in a large pot or Dutch oven over medium heat.
Add the diced onion and bell peppers to the pot. Cook, stirring occasionally, until the vegetables are softened, about 5-7 minutes.
Add the minced garlic to the pot and cook for an additional 1-2 minutes, until fragrant.
Add the ground turkey to the pot, breaking it apart with a spoon. Cook until the turkey is browned and cooked through, about 5-7 minutes.
Stir in the chili powder, ground cumin, paprika, dried oregano, cayenne pepper (if using), salt, and pepper. Cook for another 1-2 minutes to toast the spices and coat the turkey and vegetables.
Add the diced tomatoes (with their juices), tomato sauce, kidney beans, black beans, and chicken broth to the pot. Stir well to combine.

Bring the chili to a simmer, then reduce the heat to low. Cover and let the chili simmer for about 30 minutes to allow the flavors to meld together and the chili to thicken slightly.
Taste and adjust seasoning if needed, adding more salt and pepper as desired.
Serve the turkey chili hot, garnished with your favorite toppings such as shredded cheese, diced avocado, chopped cilantro, sour cream, lime wedges, or tortilla chips.
Enjoy your Turkey Chili with Beans!

This hearty and comforting dish is perfect for chilly days and makes great leftovers for lunch or dinner. It's also freezer-friendly, so you can make a big batch and store it for later enjoyment.

Greek Yogurt Parfait with Granola and Honey

Ingredients:

- 1 cup Greek yogurt (plain or flavored, depending on preference)
- 1/2 cup granola (store-bought or homemade)
- 2 tablespoons honey
- 1/2 cup mixed fresh berries (such as strawberries, blueberries, raspberries)

Instructions:

In a serving glass or bowl, layer half of the Greek yogurt at the bottom.
Sprinkle half of the granola evenly over the yogurt layer.
Drizzle 1 tablespoon of honey over the granola layer.
Add half of the mixed fresh berries on top of the honey layer.
Repeat the layers with the remaining Greek yogurt, granola, honey, and mixed fresh berries.
Serve immediately and enjoy your Greek Yogurt Parfait with Granola and Honey!

This parfait makes a nutritious and satisfying breakfast, snack, or even dessert. Feel free to customize it with your favorite fruits, nuts, or additional toppings like shredded coconut or chocolate chips.

Veggie Stir-Fry with Tofu

Ingredients:

- 1 block (about 14 ounces) firm tofu, pressed and cubed
- 2 tablespoons soy sauce
- 1 tablespoon rice vinegar
- 1 tablespoon sesame oil
- 1 tablespoon cornstarch
- 2 tablespoons vegetable oil (for cooking)
- 2 cloves garlic, minced
- 1 tablespoon fresh ginger, minced
- 1 bell pepper, thinly sliced
- 1 carrot, julienned
- 1 cup broccoli florets
- 1 cup snap peas, trimmed
- 1 cup sliced mushrooms
- Salt and pepper to taste
- Cooked rice or noodles for serving

Instructions:

In a small bowl, whisk together the soy sauce, rice vinegar, sesame oil, and cornstarch to make the sauce. Set aside.

Heat one tablespoon of vegetable oil in a large skillet or wok over medium-high heat.

Add the cubed tofu to the skillet in a single layer. Cook for 5-7 minutes, flipping occasionally, until the tofu is golden brown and crispy on all sides. Remove the tofu from the skillet and set it aside.

In the same skillet, add the remaining tablespoon of vegetable oil.

Add the minced garlic and ginger to the skillet and cook for 1-2 minutes, until fragrant.

Add the sliced bell pepper, julienned carrot, broccoli florets, snap peas, and sliced mushrooms to the skillet. Stir-fry for 5-7 minutes, or until the vegetables are tender-crisp.

Return the cooked tofu to the skillet with the vegetables.

Pour the sauce over the tofu and vegetables in the skillet. Stir well to coat everything evenly with the sauce.

Cook for an additional 2-3 minutes, stirring occasionally, until the sauce has thickened slightly and everything is heated through.
Season with salt and pepper to taste.
Serve the veggie stir-fry with tofu hot, over cooked rice or noodles.
Enjoy your delicious Veggie Stir-Fry with Tofu!

This dish is not only flavorful and satisfying but also packed with protein and vegetables, making it a nutritious option for lunch or dinner. Feel free to customize it with your favorite veggies and adjust the seasoning according to your taste preferences.

Lean Beef Tacos with Salsa and Guacamole

Ingredients:

For the lean beef filling:

- 1 lb lean ground beef
- 1 tablespoon olive oil
- 1 small onion, finely chopped
- 2 cloves garlic, minced
- 1 teaspoon ground cumin
- 1 teaspoon chili powder
- 1/2 teaspoon paprika
- Salt and pepper to taste

For the salsa:

- 2 large tomatoes, diced
- 1/2 red onion, finely chopped
- 1 jalapeño, seeded and finely chopped
- 1/4 cup chopped fresh cilantro
- Juice of 1 lime
- Salt and pepper to taste

For the guacamole:

- 2 ripe avocados
- 1/4 cup chopped red onion
- 1/4 cup chopped fresh cilantro
- Juice of 1 lime
- Salt and pepper to taste

For serving:

- 8-10 small corn or flour tortillas
- Shredded lettuce
- Shredded cheese

- Sour cream (optional)

Instructions:

Heat olive oil in a large skillet over medium heat. Add chopped onion and garlic, and sauté until softened, about 2-3 minutes.
Add lean ground beef to the skillet. Cook, breaking up the meat with a spoon, until browned and cooked through, about 5-7 minutes.
Stir in ground cumin, chili powder, paprika, salt, and pepper. Cook for an additional 1-2 minutes, until spices are fragrant. Remove from heat and set aside.
In a medium bowl, combine diced tomatoes, chopped red onion, jalapeño, chopped cilantro, lime juice, salt, and pepper to make the salsa. Mix well and set aside.
In another bowl, scoop out the flesh of ripe avocados and mash with a fork until smooth, leaving some chunks if desired. Add chopped red onion, chopped cilantro, lime juice, salt, and pepper to make the guacamole. Mix until well combined and set aside.
Warm tortillas in a dry skillet or in the microwave until heated through and pliable.
Assemble tacos by spooning some of the lean beef filling onto each tortilla. Top with shredded lettuce, salsa, guacamole, shredded cheese, and sour cream if desired.
Serve immediately and enjoy your delicious lean beef tacos with salsa and guacamole!

These tacos are perfect for a quick and satisfying weeknight dinner or for entertaining guests. Feel free to customize the toppings and adjust the seasoning to suit your taste preferences.

Whole Wheat Pasta with Chicken and Pesto

Ingredients:

For the pesto:

- 2 cups fresh basil leaves, packed
- 1/2 cup grated Parmesan cheese
- 1/3 cup pine nuts or walnuts
- 2 cloves garlic, peeled
- 1/2 cup extra virgin olive oil
- Salt and pepper to taste

For the pasta:

- 8 oz whole wheat pasta (such as spaghetti or penne)
- 2 boneless, skinless chicken breasts, cut into bite-sized pieces
- Salt and pepper to taste
- 2 tablespoons olive oil
- 2 cloves garlic, minced
- 1 cup cherry tomatoes, halved
- 1/4 cup grated Parmesan cheese (optional, for serving)
- Fresh basil leaves, for garnish (optional)

Instructions:

To make the pesto, combine the basil leaves, grated Parmesan cheese, pine nuts or walnuts, and garlic in a food processor or blender. Pulse until coarsely chopped.

With the food processor or blender running, slowly add the olive oil in a steady stream until the pesto is smooth and well combined. Season with salt and pepper to taste. Set aside.

Cook the whole wheat pasta according to the package instructions until al dente. Drain and set aside, reserving about 1/4 cup of pasta water.

Season the chicken breast pieces with salt and pepper to taste.

Heat olive oil in a large skillet over medium-high heat. Add the minced garlic and sauté for about 1 minute, until fragrant.

Add the seasoned chicken breast pieces to the skillet and cook for about 6-8 minutes, stirring occasionally, until cooked through and browned on all sides.

Add the halved cherry tomatoes to the skillet and cook for an additional 2-3 minutes, until softened.

Add the cooked whole wheat pasta to the skillet with the chicken and tomatoes. Stir in the prepared pesto until everything is evenly coated. If the pasta seems dry, add some of the reserved pasta water to loosen it up.

Cook for an additional 1-2 minutes, stirring gently, until everything is heated through.

Remove from heat and transfer the pasta with chicken and pesto to serving plates.

Serve hot, garnished with grated Parmesan cheese and fresh basil leaves if desired.

Enjoy your delicious Whole Wheat Pasta with Chicken and Pesto!

This dish is not only flavorful and satisfying but also packed with protein, fiber, and healthy fats. It's perfect for a quick and nutritious weeknight dinner or for entertaining guests. Feel free to customize the recipe by adding your favorite vegetables or using different protein sources.

Egg White Omelette with Spinach and Feta

Ingredients:

- 4 large egg whites
- 1 cup fresh spinach leaves, chopped
- 1/4 cup crumbled feta cheese
- 1 tablespoon olive oil
- Salt and pepper to taste

Instructions:

In a mixing bowl, whisk the egg whites until frothy. Season with salt and pepper to taste.
Heat olive oil in a non-stick skillet over medium heat.
Add the chopped spinach to the skillet and sauté for 1-2 minutes, until wilted.
Pour the whisked egg whites over the spinach in the skillet, spreading them evenly to cover the surface.
Cook the omelette for 2-3 minutes, or until the edges begin to set.
Sprinkle the crumbled feta cheese evenly over one half of the omelette.
Using a spatula, carefully fold the other half of the omelette over the side with the cheese, creating a half-moon shape.
Cook for another 1-2 minutes, or until the cheese is melted and the omelette is cooked through.
Slide the omelette onto a plate and serve hot.
Enjoy your Egg White Omelette with Spinach and Feta!

This omelette is light, fluffy, and packed with protein and nutrients from the egg whites, spinach, and feta cheese. It makes a satisfying and healthy breakfast or brunch option. Feel free to customize the recipe by adding other ingredients such as tomatoes, mushrooms, onions, or bell peppers.

Grilled Shrimp Skewers with Cajun Seasoning

Ingredients:

- 1 lb large shrimp, peeled and deveined
- 2 tablespoons olive oil
- 2 cloves garlic, minced
- 1 tablespoon paprika
- 1 teaspoon dried thyme
- 1 teaspoon dried oregano
- 1/2 teaspoon onion powder
- 1/2 teaspoon garlic powder
- 1/2 teaspoon cayenne pepper (adjust to taste for spice level)
- 1/2 teaspoon salt
- 1/4 teaspoon black pepper
- Wooden or metal skewers, soaked in water if using wooden skewers

Instructions:

If using wooden skewers, soak them in water for at least 30 minutes to prevent burning on the grill.
In a small bowl, mix together the olive oil, minced garlic, paprika, dried thyme, dried oregano, onion powder, garlic powder, cayenne pepper, salt, and black pepper to create the Cajun seasoning.
Pat the shrimp dry with paper towels. Thread the shrimp onto the skewers, dividing them evenly.
Brush the shrimp skewers on both sides with the Cajun seasoning mixture, ensuring they are well coated.
Preheat the grill to medium-high heat.
Place the shrimp skewers on the preheated grill. Grill for 2-3 minutes on each side, or until the shrimp are pink and opaque, and grill marks appear.
Remove the grilled shrimp skewers from the grill and transfer them to a serving platter.
Serve hot, garnished with fresh chopped parsley and lemon wedges if desired.
Enjoy your Grilled Shrimp Skewers with Cajun Seasoning!

These grilled shrimp skewers are perfect for a summer barbecue or as a quick and flavorful weeknight meal. Serve them with rice, salad, or grilled vegetables for a complete and delicious dish. Adjust the seasoning according to your taste preferences and enjoy the bold flavors of Cajun cuisine!

Sweet Potato Hash with Turkey Sausage

Ingredients:

- 2 medium sweet potatoes, peeled and diced into small cubes
- 1 tablespoon olive oil
- 1/2 teaspoon smoked paprika
- 1/2 teaspoon garlic powder
- Salt and pepper to taste
- 8 oz turkey sausage, casings removed and crumbled
- 1/2 onion, diced
- 1 bell pepper, diced
- 2 cloves garlic, minced
- 2 cups fresh spinach leaves
- Optional toppings: chopped fresh parsley, sliced green onions, hot sauce

Instructions:

In a large skillet, heat the olive oil over medium heat. Add the diced sweet potatoes to the skillet and season with smoked paprika, garlic powder, salt, and pepper. Cook, stirring occasionally, for about 10-12 minutes, or until the sweet potatoes are tender and lightly browned. Remove the sweet potatoes from the skillet and set aside.
In the same skillet, add the crumbled turkey sausage. Cook over medium heat, breaking up the sausage with a spoon, until browned and cooked through, about 6-8 minutes.
Add the diced onion and bell pepper to the skillet with the turkey sausage. Cook, stirring occasionally, for about 3-4 minutes, or until the vegetables are softened.
Add the minced garlic to the skillet and cook for an additional 1 minute, until fragrant.
Return the cooked sweet potatoes to the skillet with the sausage and vegetables. Stir to combine.
Add the fresh spinach leaves to the skillet and cook, stirring occasionally, until the spinach is wilted.
Taste and adjust seasoning with salt and pepper if needed.
Serve the sweet potato hash hot, topped with optional toppings such as chopped fresh parsley, sliced green onions, or hot sauce.
Enjoy your Sweet Potato Hash with Turkey Sausage!

This flavorful and nutritious dish is perfect for breakfast, brunch, or dinner. It's hearty, satisfying, and packed with protein and vegetables. Feel free to customize the recipe by adding other vegetables or spices according to your taste preferences.

Brown Rice Bowl with Grilled Vegetables

Ingredients:

For the Grilled Vegetables:

- 2 bell peppers (any color), sliced into strips
- 1 zucchini, sliced into rounds
- 1 yellow squash, sliced into rounds
- 1 red onion, sliced into wedges
- 2 tablespoons olive oil
- Salt and pepper to taste
- Optional: additional seasonings like garlic powder, paprika, or dried herbs

For the Brown Rice:

- 1 cup brown rice
- 2 cups water or vegetable broth
- Salt to taste

For the Bowl Assembly:

- Grilled vegetables (prepared above)
- Cooked brown rice (prepared above)
- Optional toppings: sliced avocado, crumbled feta cheese, chopped fresh herbs (such as parsley or cilantro), toasted nuts or seeds, drizzle of balsamic glaze or tahini sauce

Instructions:

Prepare the brown rice: In a medium saucepan, combine the brown rice, water or vegetable broth, and a pinch of salt. Bring to a boil over high heat, then reduce the heat to low, cover, and simmer for 40-45 minutes, or until the rice is tender and all the liquid is absorbed. Remove from heat and let it sit, covered, for 5-10 minutes before fluffing with a fork.
Preheat your grill to medium-high heat.

In a large bowl, toss the sliced bell peppers, zucchini, yellow squash, and red onion with olive oil, salt, pepper, and any additional seasonings you like.

Place the seasoned vegetables on the grill in a single layer (you may need to grill in batches depending on the size of your grill). Grill for 3-5 minutes per side, or until tender and charred in spots.

Once the vegetables are grilled, remove them from the grill and transfer to a plate.

Assemble the brown rice bowls: Divide the cooked brown rice among serving bowls. Top each bowl with a generous portion of grilled vegetables.

Add any desired toppings to the bowls, such as sliced avocado, crumbled feta cheese, chopped fresh herbs, or toasted nuts or seeds.

Serve the brown rice bowls immediately, with additional toppings or sauces on the side if desired.

Enjoy your flavorful and nutritious Brown Rice Bowl with Grilled Vegetables!

This dish is versatile and customizable, so feel free to mix and match your favorite vegetables and toppings to create your perfect bowl. It's a great option for a healthy and satisfying lunch or dinner.

Spinach and Berry Smoothie with Protein Powder

Ingredients:

- 1 cup fresh spinach leaves
- 1/2 cup mixed berries (such as strawberries, blueberries, raspberries)
- 1 ripe banana
- 1 scoop (about 30g) vanilla or berry-flavored protein powder
- 1 cup unsweetened almond milk or your preferred milk
- 1 tablespoon honey or maple syrup (optional, for added sweetness)
- Ice cubes (optional, for a colder smoothie)

Instructions:

Place the fresh spinach leaves, mixed berries, ripe banana, protein powder, almond milk, and honey or maple syrup (if using) in a blender.
If you prefer a colder smoothie, add a handful of ice cubes to the blender as well.
Blend on high speed until smooth and creamy, scraping down the sides of the blender as needed.
Taste the smoothie and adjust sweetness if needed by adding more honey or maple syrup.
Pour the smoothie into glasses and serve immediately.
Enjoy your refreshing Spinach and Berry Smoothie with Protein Powder!

This smoothie is not only delicious and satisfying but also packed with vitamins, minerals, fiber, and protein. It's perfect for a quick and nutritious breakfast or snack, and the addition of protein powder makes it an excellent post-workout recovery drink. Feel free to customize the recipe by using your favorite berries or swapping the protein powder flavor to suit your taste preferences.

Lentil Soup with Kale and Carrots

Ingredients:

- 1 cup dried lentils, rinsed and drained
- 1 tablespoon olive oil
- 1 onion, diced
- 2 carrots, diced
- 2 cloves garlic, minced
- 6 cups vegetable broth or water
- 1 teaspoon ground cumin
- 1/2 teaspoon smoked paprika
- 1/2 teaspoon dried thyme
- Salt and pepper to taste
- 2 cups chopped kale leaves, tough stems removed
- Juice of 1 lemon
- Optional toppings: chopped fresh parsley, grated Parmesan cheese, a dollop of Greek yogurt

Instructions:

Heat the olive oil in a large pot over medium heat. Add the diced onion and carrots to the pot and cook for 5-7 minutes, or until softened.
Add the minced garlic to the pot and cook for an additional 1 minute, until fragrant.
Stir in the rinsed lentils, vegetable broth or water, ground cumin, smoked paprika, dried thyme, salt, and pepper.
Bring the soup to a boil, then reduce the heat to low. Cover and simmer for 20-25 minutes, or until the lentils are tender.
Once the lentils are cooked, stir in the chopped kale leaves and lemon juice. Cook for an additional 5 minutes, or until the kale is wilted and tender.
Taste the soup and adjust seasoning with more salt and pepper if needed.
Ladle the lentil soup into bowls and garnish with optional toppings such as chopped fresh parsley, grated Parmesan cheese, or a dollop of Greek yogurt.
Serve hot and enjoy your hearty Lentil Soup with Kale and Carrots!

This soup is nutritious, flavorful, and perfect for a cozy meal on a chilly day. It's packed with protein, fiber, vitamins, and minerals from the lentils, kale, and carrots. Plus, it's easy to customize with your favorite herbs and spices. Feel free to experiment with different variations to suit your taste preferences.

Baked Cod with Lemon and Garlic

Ingredients:

- 4 cod fillets (about 6 ounces each)
- 2 tablespoons olive oil
- 4 cloves garlic, minced
- Zest of 1 lemon
- Juice of 1 lemon
- Salt and pepper to taste
- Fresh parsley, chopped, for garnish
- Lemon slices, for serving

Instructions:

Preheat your oven to 400°F (200°C). Lightly grease a baking dish with olive oil or line it with parchment paper.

Place the cod fillets in the prepared baking dish, arranging them in a single layer.

In a small bowl, mix together the olive oil, minced garlic, lemon zest, and lemon juice.

Drizzle the garlic-lemon mixture evenly over the cod fillets, making sure each fillet is well coated. Use your hands or a brush to spread the mixture evenly.

Season the cod fillets with salt and pepper to taste.

Bake the cod in the preheated oven for 12-15 minutes, or until the fish is opaque and flakes easily with a fork.

Remove the baked cod from the oven and garnish with chopped fresh parsley.

Serve hot, with lemon slices on the side for squeezing over the fish.

Enjoy your flavorful Baked Cod with Lemon and Garlic!

This dish is light, healthy, and bursting with fresh flavors. It's perfect for a quick weeknight dinner yet elegant enough for entertaining guests. Serve the baked cod with your favorite sides, such as steamed vegetables, rice, or a salad, for a complete and satisfying meal.

Quinoa Stuffed Bell Peppers

Ingredients:

- 4 large bell peppers (any color), tops removed and seeds removed
- 1 cup quinoa, rinsed
- 2 cups vegetable broth or water
- 1 tablespoon olive oil
- 1 small onion, diced
- 2 cloves garlic, minced
- 1 carrot, diced
- 1 zucchini, diced
- 1 cup corn kernels (fresh, frozen, or canned)
- 1 cup cooked black beans (or canned, drained and rinsed)
- 1 teaspoon ground cumin
- 1 teaspoon chili powder
- Salt and pepper to taste
- 1 cup shredded cheese (cheddar, mozzarella, or your choice)
- Optional toppings: chopped fresh cilantro, sliced green onions, avocado slices, sour cream or Greek yogurt

Instructions:

Preheat your oven to 375°F (190°C). Lightly grease a baking dish large enough to hold the bell peppers upright.

In a medium saucepan, bring the vegetable broth or water to a boil. Add the rinsed quinoa, reduce the heat to low, cover, and simmer for about 15-20 minutes, or until the quinoa is cooked and fluffy and the liquid is absorbed. Remove from heat and set aside.

While the quinoa is cooking, heat the olive oil in a large skillet over medium heat. Add the diced onion and garlic, and cook for 2-3 minutes, or until softened and fragrant.

Add the diced carrot and zucchini to the skillet, and cook for another 3-4 minutes, or until the vegetables are tender.

Stir in the corn kernels and black beans, and cook for an additional 2 minutes to heat through.

Add the cooked quinoa to the skillet with the vegetables, and sprinkle with ground cumin, chili powder, salt, and pepper. Stir well to combine and cook for another 2-3 minutes to allow the flavors to meld.

Remove the skillet from the heat, and stir in half of the shredded cheese until melted and combined with the quinoa mixture.

Spoon the quinoa mixture into the hollowed-out bell peppers, pressing down gently to fill them completely.

Place the stuffed bell peppers upright in the prepared baking dish. Sprinkle the remaining shredded cheese on top of each stuffed pepper.

Cover the baking dish with aluminum foil, and bake in the preheated oven for 25-30 minutes, or until the bell peppers are tender and the filling is heated through.

Remove the foil, and bake for an additional 5-10 minutes, or until the cheese is bubbly and lightly golden.

Remove from the oven and let cool for a few minutes before serving.

Garnish the stuffed bell peppers with optional toppings such as chopped fresh cilantro, sliced green onions, avocado slices, and a dollop of sour cream or Greek yogurt.

Serve hot and enjoy your delicious Quinoa Stuffed Bell Peppers!

These stuffed bell peppers are nutritious, flavorful, and versatile. They make a satisfying vegetarian main dish or a hearty side dish for any meal. Feel free to customize the recipe with your favorite vegetables, spices, or toppings.

Oatmeal with Almond Butter and Banana

Ingredients:

- 1/2 cup rolled oats
- 1 cup water or milk of your choice (such as almond milk, cow's milk, or soy milk)
- Pinch of salt
- 1 tablespoon almond butter
- 1 ripe banana, sliced
- Optional toppings: drizzle of honey or maple syrup, sprinkle of cinnamon, chopped nuts or seeds, shredded coconut, or additional sliced fruit

Instructions:

In a small saucepan, bring the water or milk to a gentle boil over medium heat. Stir in the rolled oats and a pinch of salt.

Reduce the heat to low and simmer, stirring occasionally, for about 5 minutes or until the oatmeal reaches your desired consistency. If you prefer thicker oatmeal, simmer for a few minutes longer.

Once the oatmeal is cooked to your liking, remove the saucepan from the heat. Transfer the cooked oatmeal to a serving bowl.

Stir in the almond butter until it's melted and evenly distributed throughout the oatmeal.

Top the oatmeal with sliced banana.

If desired, drizzle with honey or maple syrup for added sweetness and sprinkle with cinnamon for extra flavor.

You can also add additional toppings such as chopped nuts or seeds, shredded coconut, or more sliced fruit.

Serve hot and enjoy your comforting and nutritious Oatmeal with Almond Butter and Banana!

This oatmeal recipe is quick, easy, and customizable to your taste preferences. It's a wholesome breakfast option that will keep you satisfied and energized throughout the morning. Feel free to adjust the ingredients and toppings according to what you have on hand or your personal preferences.

Chicken and Vegetable Kabobs

Ingredients:

- 1 lb boneless, skinless chicken breasts, cut into bite-sized pieces
- 2 bell peppers (any color), cut into chunks
- 1 red onion, cut into chunks
- 1 zucchini, sliced into rounds
- 1 yellow squash, sliced into rounds
- 8-10 cherry tomatoes
- Wooden or metal skewers
- Olive oil, for brushing
- Salt and pepper to taste
- Optional marinade: your favorite marinade or a simple mixture of olive oil, lemon juice, garlic, and herbs

Instructions:

If using wooden skewers, soak them in water for at least 30 minutes to prevent burning on the grill.
In a bowl, combine the chicken pieces with your choice of marinade (if using). Toss to coat evenly and let marinate for at least 30 minutes, or up to 4 hours in the refrigerator.
Preheat your grill to medium-high heat.
Thread the marinated chicken pieces and prepared vegetables onto the skewers, alternating between chicken and vegetables.
Brush the assembled kabobs with olive oil and season with salt and pepper to taste.
Place the kabobs on the preheated grill and cook for 10-12 minutes, turning occasionally, until the chicken is cooked through and the vegetables are tender and lightly charred.
Once cooked, remove the kabobs from the grill and let them rest for a few minutes.
Serve the chicken and vegetable kabobs hot, with your favorite side dishes such as rice, quinoa, or a fresh salad.
Enjoy your delicious and flavorful Chicken and Vegetable Kabobs!

These kabobs are perfect for a summer barbecue or a quick and healthy weeknight dinner. Feel free to customize the recipe by using your favorite vegetables or adding extra seasoning to the chicken. You can also serve them with your favorite dipping sauce or tzatziki for extra flavor.

Greek Salad with Grilled Chicken

Ingredients:

For the Grilled Chicken:

- 1 lb boneless, skinless chicken breasts
- 2 tablespoons olive oil
- 2 cloves garlic, minced
- 1 teaspoon dried oregano
- 1/2 teaspoon dried thyme
- Salt and pepper to taste

For the Greek Salad:

- 4 cups mixed salad greens (such as lettuce, spinach, or arugula)
- 1 cucumber, diced
- 1 bell pepper (any color), diced
- 1 cup cherry tomatoes, halved
- 1/2 red onion, thinly sliced
- 1/2 cup Kalamata olives, pitted
- 1/2 cup crumbled feta cheese
- Optional additional toppings: sliced radishes, chopped fresh parsley, sliced avocado

For the Dressing:

- 1/4 cup extra virgin olive oil
- 2 tablespoons red wine vinegar
- 1 clove garlic, minced
- 1 teaspoon dried oregano
- Salt and pepper to taste

Instructions:

In a small bowl, whisk together the olive oil, minced garlic, dried oregano, dried thyme, salt, and pepper to make the marinade for the grilled chicken.
Place the chicken breasts in a shallow dish or resealable plastic bag, and pour the marinade over the chicken. Make sure the chicken is evenly coated. Cover or

seal the dish/bag and marinate in the refrigerator for at least 30 minutes, or up to 4 hours.

Preheat your grill to medium-high heat. Remove the chicken from the marinade and discard any excess marinade.

Grill the chicken breasts for 6-8 minutes per side, or until cooked through and no longer pink in the center. Cooking time may vary depending on the thickness of the chicken breasts. Remove from the grill and let them rest for a few minutes before slicing.

While the chicken is grilling, prepare the Greek salad. In a large salad bowl, combine the mixed salad greens, diced cucumber, diced bell pepper, halved cherry tomatoes, thinly sliced red onion, Kalamata olives, and crumbled feta cheese. Toss gently to combine.

In a small bowl, whisk together the ingredients for the dressing: extra virgin olive oil, red wine vinegar, minced garlic, dried oregano, salt, and pepper.

Drizzle the dressing over the salad and toss until everything is evenly coated.

Divide the Greek salad among serving plates. Top each salad with sliced grilled chicken.

Garnish the salads with optional toppings such as sliced radishes, chopped fresh parsley, or sliced avocado.

Serve immediately and enjoy your delicious Greek Salad with Grilled Chicken!

This salad is fresh, colorful, and packed with Mediterranean flavors. It's perfect for a light and healthy lunch or dinner, and the grilled chicken adds protein to make it more satisfying. Feel free to customize the salad with your favorite vegetables or add a squeeze of lemon juice for extra brightness.

Turkey Meatballs with Marinara Sauce

Ingredients:

For the Turkey Meatballs:

- 1 lb ground turkey
- 1/2 cup breadcrumbs
- 1/4 cup grated Parmesan cheese
- 1 egg
- 2 cloves garlic, minced
- 2 tablespoons fresh parsley, chopped
- 1 teaspoon dried oregano
- 1/2 teaspoon dried basil
- Salt and pepper to taste
- Olive oil, for cooking

For the Marinara Sauce:

- 2 tablespoons olive oil
- 1 onion, diced
- 2 cloves garlic, minced
- 1 can (28 oz) crushed tomatoes
- 1 teaspoon dried oregano
- 1/2 teaspoon dried basil
- Salt and pepper to taste
- Optional: pinch of red pepper flakes for a hint of heat

Instructions:

Preheat your oven to 375°F (190°C). Line a baking sheet with parchment paper or lightly grease it with olive oil.
In a large mixing bowl, combine ground turkey, breadcrumbs, grated Parmesan cheese, egg, minced garlic, chopped parsley, dried oregano, dried basil, salt, and pepper. Mix until all ingredients are well combined.
Shape the turkey mixture into meatballs, about 1 to 1.5 inches in diameter, and place them on the prepared baking sheet.

Bake the turkey meatballs in the preheated oven for 20-25 minutes, or until they are cooked through and golden brown on the outside.

While the meatballs are baking, prepare the marinara sauce. In a large skillet, heat olive oil over medium heat. Add diced onion and minced garlic, and sauté until softened and fragrant, about 3-4 minutes.

Add crushed tomatoes, dried oregano, dried basil, salt, pepper, and optional red pepper flakes to the skillet. Stir to combine.

Bring the sauce to a simmer, then reduce the heat to low and let it cook for about 15-20 minutes, stirring occasionally, to allow the flavors to meld and the sauce to thicken slightly.

Once the meatballs are done baking and the marinara sauce is ready, add the meatballs to the skillet with the marinara sauce, and gently stir to coat them with the sauce.

Let the meatballs simmer in the sauce for a few minutes to absorb the flavors.

Serve the turkey meatballs with marinara sauce hot, over cooked pasta, zucchini noodles, or with crusty bread for dipping.

Garnish with additional grated Parmesan cheese and chopped fresh parsley if desired.

Enjoy your delicious Turkey Meatballs with Marinara Sauce!

These turkey meatballs are juicy, flavorful, and healthier than traditional beef meatballs.

The marinara sauce adds a rich and savory flavor that complements the meatballs

perfectly. It's a comforting and satisfying dish that the whole family will love!

Whole Wheat Wrap with Turkey, Hummus, and Veggies

Ingredients:

- 1 whole wheat tortilla or wrap
- 2-3 slices of deli turkey breast
- 2 tablespoons hummus (your choice of flavor)
- 1/4 cup shredded carrots
- 1/4 cup sliced cucumber
- 1/4 cup baby spinach leaves
- 1/4 avocado, sliced
- Optional: sliced bell peppers, cherry tomatoes, red onion, or any other favorite veggies
- Optional: a squeeze of lemon juice or a drizzle of balsamic glaze for extra flavor

Instructions:

Lay the whole wheat tortilla or wrap flat on a clean surface.
Spread the hummus evenly over the surface of the tortilla.
Arrange the deli turkey slices in a single layer on top of the hummus.
Layer the shredded carrots, sliced cucumber, baby spinach leaves, and avocado slices on top of the turkey slices.
Add any additional veggies of your choice, such as sliced bell peppers, cherry tomatoes, or red onion.
If desired, squeeze a little lemon juice over the veggies or drizzle with balsamic glaze for extra flavor.
Starting from one end, tightly roll up the wrap, folding in the sides as you go, to create a compact cylinder.
Cut the wrap in half diagonally or into smaller pinwheels if preferred.
Serve immediately, or wrap the halves/pinwheels in parchment paper or foil for a convenient grab-and-go meal.
Enjoy your delicious and nutritious Whole Wheat Wrap with Turkey, Hummus, and Veggies!

This wrap is packed with protein, fiber, vitamins, and minerals, making it a satisfying and balanced meal option for lunch or a light dinner. Feel free to customize the ingredients based on your preferences or what you have on hand. You can also add a sprinkle of feta cheese or a drizzle of hot sauce for extra flavor.

Cottage Cheese and Fruit Bowl

Ingredients:

- 1/2 cup cottage cheese
- 1/2 cup mixed fresh fruit (such as berries, sliced banana, diced pineapple, or sliced peaches)
- 1 tablespoon chopped nuts (such as almonds, walnuts, or pecans)
- Optional: drizzle of honey or maple syrup, sprinkle of cinnamon

Instructions:

Spoon the cottage cheese into a serving bowl.
Arrange the mixed fresh fruit on top of the cottage cheese.
Sprinkle the chopped nuts over the fruit.
If desired, drizzle the cottage cheese and fruit bowl with honey or maple syrup for added sweetness.
Optional: sprinkle with cinnamon for extra flavor.
Serve immediately and enjoy your delicious Cottage Cheese and Fruit Bowl!

This simple and nutritious dish makes a satisfying breakfast, snack, or light dessert. It's packed with protein from the cottage cheese, vitamins, minerals, and fiber from the fresh fruit, and healthy fats from the nuts. Feel free to customize the recipe with your favorite fruits, nuts, or additional toppings such as granola or coconut flakes.

Tuna Salad with Avocado and Spinach

Ingredients:

- 1 can (5 oz) tuna, drained
- 1 ripe avocado, diced
- 1 cup fresh spinach leaves
- 1/4 cup diced red onion
- 1/4 cup diced celery
- 2 tablespoons chopped fresh parsley
- 1 tablespoon lemon juice
- 1 tablespoon olive oil
- Salt and pepper to taste
- Optional: sliced cherry tomatoes, cucumber, or any other desired veggies
- Optional: whole wheat bread, wraps, or crackers for serving

Instructions:

In a large mixing bowl, combine the drained tuna, diced avocado, fresh spinach leaves, diced red onion, diced celery, and chopped fresh parsley.
Drizzle the lemon juice and olive oil over the ingredients in the bowl.
Season the tuna salad with salt and pepper to taste.
Gently toss all the ingredients together until well combined, taking care not to mash the avocado too much.
If desired, add sliced cherry tomatoes, cucumber, or any other desired veggies to the tuna salad and toss gently to incorporate.
Serve the tuna salad immediately on its own, or as a filling for sandwiches, wraps, or served with whole wheat crackers.
Enjoy your delicious and nutritious Tuna Salad with Avocado and Spinach!

This tuna salad is packed with protein, healthy fats, and vitamins from the tuna, avocado, and spinach. It's quick and easy to make and can be enjoyed for a light lunch, dinner, or snack. Feel free to customize the recipe with your favorite ingredients or add a sprinkle of herbs or a squeeze of lime juice for extra flavor.

Black Bean and Corn Quesadillas

Ingredients:

- 1 can (15 oz) black beans, drained and rinsed
- 1 cup frozen corn kernels, thawed
- 1/2 red bell pepper, diced
- 1/2 green bell pepper, diced
- 1/4 cup diced red onion
- 1 teaspoon ground cumin
- 1 teaspoon chili powder
- Salt and pepper to taste
- 2 cups shredded cheese (such as cheddar, Monterey Jack, or a Mexican blend)
- 4 large flour tortillas
- Olive oil or cooking spray, for cooking
- Optional toppings: salsa, guacamole, sour cream, chopped cilantro, sliced jalapeños

Instructions:

In a large mixing bowl, combine the black beans, corn kernels, diced bell peppers, diced red onion, ground cumin, chili powder, salt, and pepper. Mix well to combine.
Heat a large skillet over medium heat. Place one flour tortilla in the skillet and sprinkle a quarter of the shredded cheese evenly over one half of the tortilla.
Spoon a quarter of the black bean and corn mixture over the cheese.
Fold the other half of the tortilla over the filling to create a half-moon shape.
Cook the quesadilla for 2-3 minutes on each side, or until the tortilla is golden brown and crispy and the cheese is melted.
Remove the cooked quesadilla from the skillet and repeat the process with the remaining tortillas and filling ingredients.
Once all the quesadillas are cooked, transfer them to a cutting board and let them cool for a minute.
Use a sharp knife to slice each quesadilla into wedges.
Serve the Black Bean and Corn Quesadillas hot, with your favorite toppings such as salsa, guacamole, sour cream, chopped cilantro, or sliced jalapeños on the side.
Enjoy your delicious and flavorful Black Bean and Corn Quesadillas!

These quesadillas are perfect for a quick and easy meal or snack. They're packed with protein, fiber, and flavor from the black beans, corn, and spices. Feel free to customize the recipe by adding other ingredients such as diced tomatoes, chopped cilantro, or sliced avocado.

Baked Sweet Potato Fries

Ingredients:

- 2 large sweet potatoes
- 2 tablespoons olive oil
- 1 teaspoon paprika
- 1/2 teaspoon garlic powder
- 1/2 teaspoon onion powder
- 1/2 teaspoon salt
- 1/4 teaspoon black pepper
- Optional: a pinch of cayenne pepper for a spicy kick
- Optional: chopped fresh parsley for garnish

Instructions:

Preheat your oven to 425°F (220°C). Line a large baking sheet with parchment paper or aluminum foil and lightly grease with cooking spray or olive oil.
Wash the sweet potatoes well and pat them dry with a paper towel. Leave the skin on for extra fiber and nutrients.
Cut the sweet potatoes into thin strips, about 1/4 to 1/2 inch thick. Try to make them as uniform in size as possible so they cook evenly.
In a large bowl, toss the sweet potato strips with olive oil until evenly coated.
In a small bowl, mix together the paprika, garlic powder, onion powder, salt, pepper, and cayenne pepper (if using).
Sprinkle the spice mixture over the sweet potato strips and toss until they are evenly coated with the spices.
Arrange the sweet potato strips in a single layer on the prepared baking sheet, making sure they are not touching or overlapping.
Bake in the preheated oven for 20-25 minutes, flipping halfway through, until the sweet potato fries are golden brown and crispy on the outside, and tender on the inside.
Once done, remove the baking sheet from the oven and let the sweet potato fries cool slightly.
Garnish with chopped fresh parsley if desired, and serve the baked sweet potato fries hot with your favorite dipping sauce, such as ketchup, aioli, or Greek yogurt mixed with herbs.
Enjoy your delicious and nutritious Baked Sweet Potato Fries!

These baked sweet potato fries are crispy, flavorful, and addictive. They make a great side dish or snack, and they're packed with vitamins, minerals, and fiber from the sweet potatoes. Feel free to adjust the seasoning to your taste preferences, and experiment with different dipping sauces for added variety.

Chicken and Vegetable Stir-Fry with Brown Rice

Ingredients:

For the Stir-Fry Sauce:

- 1/4 cup soy sauce (or tamari for gluten-free option)
- 2 tablespoons oyster sauce
- 1 tablespoon rice vinegar
- 1 tablespoon honey or brown sugar
- 1 teaspoon sesame oil
- 2 cloves garlic, minced
- 1 teaspoon minced ginger
- 1 tablespoon cornstarch (optional, for thickening)

For the Stir-Fry:

- 1 lb boneless, skinless chicken breasts, cut into thin strips
- 2 tablespoons vegetable oil, divided
- 1 bell pepper, thinly sliced
- 1 cup broccoli florets
- 1 carrot, thinly sliced
- 1 cup snap peas or snow peas
- 1 cup sliced mushrooms
- 4 cups cooked brown rice (about 2 cups uncooked)
- Sesame seeds and chopped green onions for garnish (optional)

Instructions:

In a small bowl, whisk together all the ingredients for the stir-fry sauce: soy sauce, oyster sauce, rice vinegar, honey or brown sugar, sesame oil, minced garlic, and minced ginger. If you prefer a thicker sauce, you can add cornstarch dissolved in a little water to the sauce mixture.

In a large skillet or wok, heat 1 tablespoon of vegetable oil over medium-high heat. Add the sliced chicken breast strips and stir-fry until cooked through and lightly browned. Remove the chicken from the skillet and set aside.

In the same skillet, add the remaining tablespoon of vegetable oil. Add the sliced bell pepper, broccoli florets, sliced carrot, snap peas or snow peas, and sliced mushrooms. Stir-fry for 3-4 minutes, or until the vegetables are crisp-tender.

Return the cooked chicken to the skillet with the vegetables.
Pour the prepared stir-fry sauce over the chicken and vegetables in the skillet. Stir well to coat everything evenly in the sauce.
Cook for an additional 2-3 minutes, or until the sauce is heated through and slightly thickened.
Serve the chicken and vegetable stir-fry hot over cooked brown rice.
Garnish with sesame seeds and chopped green onions if desired.
Enjoy your delicious Chicken and Vegetable Stir-Fry with Brown Rice!

This stir-fry is packed with flavor, protein, and healthy vegetables, and it's perfect for a quick and nutritious weeknight dinner. You can customize the recipe by using your favorite vegetables or adding different proteins such as tofu or shrimp. Feel free to adjust the seasoning to your taste preferences, and enjoy!

Grilled Steak with Chimichurri Sauce

Ingredients:

For the Steak:

- 2 ribeye steaks, about 1 inch thick
- Salt and black pepper to taste
- Olive oil for grilling

For the Chimichurri Sauce:

- 1 cup fresh parsley leaves, finely chopped
- 1/4 cup fresh cilantro leaves, finely chopped
- 3 cloves garlic, minced
- 1 shallot, finely chopped
- 1/4 cup red wine vinegar
- 1/2 cup extra virgin olive oil
- 1 teaspoon dried oregano
- 1/2 teaspoon red pepper flakes (adjust to taste)
- Salt and black pepper to taste

Instructions:

Preheat your grill to medium-high heat.
Season the ribeye steaks generously with salt and black pepper on both sides.
Brush the grill grates with olive oil to prevent sticking.
Place the seasoned steaks on the preheated grill and cook for about 4-5 minutes per side for medium-rare doneness, or adjust the cooking time according to your preference and the thickness of the steaks.
While the steaks are grilling, prepare the chimichurri sauce. In a medium bowl, combine the finely chopped parsley, cilantro, minced garlic, chopped shallot, red wine vinegar, extra virgin olive oil, dried oregano, and red pepper flakes. Season with salt and black pepper to taste. Stir well to combine.
Once the steaks are cooked to your desired level of doneness, remove them from the grill and let them rest for a few minutes on a cutting board.
Slice the grilled steaks against the grain into thin slices.
Serve the sliced steak hot, drizzled with the chimichurri sauce on top or on the side.

Enjoy your delicious Grilled Steak with Chimichurri Sauce!

This dish is perfect for a backyard barbecue or a special dinner at home. The tender and juicy grilled steak pairs perfectly with the fresh and tangy chimichurri sauce, creating a burst of flavors with every bite. Serve the steak with your favorite side dishes such as grilled vegetables, roasted potatoes, or a crisp salad for a complete meal.

Veggie Frittata with Goat Cheese

Ingredients:

- 8 large eggs
- 1/4 cup milk or cream
- Salt and pepper to taste
- 2 tablespoons olive oil
- 1 small onion, diced
- 1 bell pepper, diced
- 1 cup sliced mushrooms
- 2 cups baby spinach leaves
- 1/4 cup crumbled goat cheese
- Optional: chopped fresh herbs such as parsley, thyme, or chives for garnish

Instructions:

Preheat your oven to 350°F (175°C).
In a large mixing bowl, whisk together the eggs and milk or cream. Season with salt and pepper to taste. Set aside.
Heat olive oil in an oven-safe skillet over medium heat. Add the diced onion and cook until softened, about 3-4 minutes.
Add the diced bell pepper and sliced mushrooms to the skillet. Cook, stirring occasionally, until the vegetables are tender, about 5 minutes.
Add the baby spinach leaves to the skillet and cook until wilted, about 1-2 minutes.
Pour the egg mixture evenly over the cooked vegetables in the skillet. Use a spatula to gently stir the mixture, distributing the vegetables evenly.
Sprinkle the crumbled goat cheese over the top of the frittata mixture.
Transfer the skillet to the preheated oven and bake for 15-20 minutes, or until the frittata is set in the center and the edges are golden brown.
Once done, remove the skillet from the oven and let the frittata cool for a few minutes.
Sprinkle chopped fresh herbs over the top for garnish, if desired.
Slice the frittata into wedges and serve hot or at room temperature.
Enjoy your delicious Veggie Frittata with Goat Cheese!

This frittata is versatile and perfect for any meal of the day. It's packed with nutritious vegetables and creamy goat cheese, making it a satisfying and flavorful dish. Serve it for breakfast, brunch, lunch, or dinner, accompanied by a side salad or some crusty bread for a complete meal. leftovers can be stored in the refrigerator for a few days and reheated as needed.

Quinoa and Black Bean Salad

Ingredients:

- 1 cup quinoa, rinsed
- 2 cups water or vegetable broth
- 1 can (15 oz) black beans, drained and rinsed
- 1 red bell pepper, diced
- 1 cup cherry tomatoes, halved
- 1/2 cup diced cucumber
- 1/4 cup chopped fresh cilantro
- 2 green onions, thinly sliced
- Juice of 1 lime
- 2 tablespoons extra virgin olive oil
- 1 teaspoon ground cumin
- Salt and pepper to taste
- Optional: avocado slices, crumbled feta cheese, sliced jalapeños for garnish

Instructions:

In a medium saucepan, combine the quinoa and water or vegetable broth. Bring to a boil over medium-high heat.
Reduce the heat to low, cover, and simmer for about 15 minutes, or until the quinoa is cooked and the liquid is absorbed. Remove from heat and let it cool slightly.
In a large mixing bowl, combine the cooked quinoa, black beans, diced red bell pepper, cherry tomatoes, diced cucumber, chopped cilantro, and sliced green onions.
In a small bowl, whisk together the lime juice, extra virgin olive oil, ground cumin, salt, and pepper to make the dressing.
Pour the dressing over the quinoa and black bean mixture in the bowl. Toss gently to coat everything evenly.
Taste and adjust the seasoning, adding more salt, pepper, or lime juice if needed.
Transfer the quinoa and black bean salad to a serving dish.
If desired, garnish with avocado slices, crumbled feta cheese, or sliced jalapeños.
Serve the salad chilled or at room temperature.
Enjoy your delicious and nutritious Quinoa and Black Bean Salad!

This salad is packed with protein, fiber, vitamins, and minerals, making it a wholesome and satisfying meal on its own or as a side dish. It's perfect for meal prep, picnics, potlucks, or any occasion. Feel free to customize the recipe by adding your favorite vegetables or herbs, or adjust the dressing to suit your taste preferences.

Greek Yogurt Chicken Salad

Ingredients:

- 2 cups cooked chicken breast, shredded or diced
- 1/2 cup plain Greek yogurt
- 1/4 cup diced cucumber
- 1/4 cup diced red bell pepper
- 1/4 cup diced celery
- 2 tablespoons diced red onion
- 2 tablespoons chopped fresh parsley
- 1 tablespoon lemon juice
- 1 tablespoon Dijon mustard
- 1 clove garlic, minced
- Salt and pepper to taste
- Optional: chopped walnuts, dried cranberries, or sliced grapes for added texture and sweetness

Instructions:

In a large mixing bowl, combine the cooked chicken breast, plain Greek yogurt, diced cucumber, diced red bell pepper, diced celery, diced red onion, chopped fresh parsley, lemon juice, Dijon mustard, and minced garlic.
Season the mixture with salt and pepper to taste.
Optional: Add chopped walnuts, dried cranberries, or sliced grapes to the chicken salad for added texture and sweetness. Mix well to combine.
Once all the ingredients are well combined, taste the chicken salad and adjust the seasoning if needed.
Cover the bowl and refrigerate the chicken salad for at least 30 minutes to allow the flavors to meld together.
Serve the Greek Yogurt Chicken Salad chilled, as a filling for sandwiches, wraps, or lettuce cups, or as a topping for salads.
Enjoy your delicious and creamy Greek Yogurt Chicken Salad!

This chicken salad is creamy, flavorful, and packed with protein. The Greek yogurt adds a tangy and creamy texture while keeping the dish light and healthy. Feel free to customize the recipe by adding your favorite ingredients such as chopped nuts, dried fruit, or fresh herbs. It's perfect for meal prep, picnics, lunches, or any occasion where you need a quick and satisfying dish.

Spaghetti Squash with Turkey Bolognese

Ingredients:

For the Spaghetti Squash:

- 1 large spaghetti squash
- Olive oil
- Salt and pepper

For the Turkey Bolognese:

- 1 lb ground turkey
- 1 tablespoon olive oil
- 1 onion, diced
- 2 cloves garlic, minced
- 1 carrot, diced
- 1 celery stalk, diced
- 1 can (14 oz) crushed tomatoes
- 1 can (6 oz) tomato paste
- 1/2 cup chicken or vegetable broth
- 1 teaspoon dried oregano
- 1 teaspoon dried basil
- Salt and pepper to taste
- Optional: grated Parmesan cheese and chopped fresh basil for garnish

Instructions:

Preheat your oven to 400°F (200°C).
Cut the spaghetti squash in half lengthwise and scoop out the seeds.
Brush the inside of each half with olive oil and sprinkle with salt and pepper.
Place the squash halves, cut side down, on a baking sheet lined with parchment paper.
Roast in the preheated oven for 35-45 minutes, or until the squash is tender and the strands easily separate when scraped with a fork.
While the squash is roasting, prepare the Turkey Bolognese sauce. In a large skillet, heat the olive oil over medium heat.

Add the diced onion, minced garlic, diced carrot, and diced celery. Cook until the vegetables are softened, about 5 minutes.

Add the ground turkey to the skillet and cook until browned, breaking it up with a spoon as it cooks.

Stir in the crushed tomatoes, tomato paste, chicken or vegetable broth, dried oregano, dried basil, salt, and pepper.

Bring the sauce to a simmer and let it cook for 15-20 minutes, stirring occasionally, until the flavors meld together and the sauce thickens slightly.

Once the spaghetti squash is done roasting, use a fork to scrape the flesh into strands.

Serve the spaghetti squash topped with the Turkey Bolognese sauce.

Garnish with grated Parmesan cheese and chopped fresh basil, if desired.

Enjoy your delicious Spaghetti Squash with Turkey Bolognese!

This dish is a healthy and satisfying alternative to traditional pasta dishes. The spaghetti squash provides a low-carb and nutrient-rich base, while the turkey bolognese is flavorful and packed with protein. It's perfect for a comforting dinner any night of the week.

Protein Smoothie Bowl with Berries and Almond Milk

Ingredients:

- 1 cup mixed berries (such as strawberries, blueberries, raspberries)
- 1 frozen banana, sliced
- 1/2 cup unsweetened almond milk (or any milk of your choice)
- 1 scoop of your favorite protein powder (vanilla or unflavored works well)
- Optional toppings: sliced fresh fruit, granola, nuts, seeds, shredded coconut, honey or maple syrup for sweetness

Instructions:

> In a blender, combine the mixed berries, frozen banana slices, almond milk, and protein powder.
> Blend until smooth and creamy. If the mixture is too thick, you can add more almond milk as needed to reach your desired consistency.
> Once the smoothie is well blended, pour it into a bowl.
> Arrange your desired toppings on top of the smoothie bowl. You can be creative and use a variety of toppings to add texture and flavor.
> Optional: Drizzle honey or maple syrup over the top for extra sweetness, if desired.
> Serve immediately and enjoy your refreshing and nutritious Protein Smoothie Bowl with Berries and Almond Milk!

This smoothie bowl is packed with protein, fiber, vitamins, and antioxidants from the berries and almond milk, making it a healthy and satisfying breakfast or snack option. Feel free to customize the recipe with your favorite fruits, protein powder flavors, and toppings to suit your taste preferences.

Teriyaki Salmon with Stir-Fried Vegetables

Ingredients:

For the Teriyaki Salmon:

- 2 salmon fillets
- 1/4 cup soy sauce
- 2 tablespoons honey
- 2 tablespoons rice vinegar
- 1 tablespoon sesame oil
- 2 cloves garlic, minced
- 1 teaspoon grated ginger
- 1 tablespoon cornstarch (optional, for thickening)
- Sesame seeds and chopped green onions for garnish (optional)

For the Stir-Fried Vegetables:

- 2 cups mixed vegetables (such as bell peppers, broccoli, carrots, snap peas)
- 1 tablespoon vegetable oil
- 2 cloves garlic, minced
- 1 teaspoon grated ginger
- 2 tablespoons soy sauce
- 1 tablespoon rice vinegar
- 1 teaspoon sesame oil
- Salt and pepper to taste

Instructions:

In a small bowl, whisk together the soy sauce, honey, rice vinegar, sesame oil, minced garlic, and grated ginger to make the teriyaki sauce. If you prefer a thicker sauce, you can add cornstarch dissolved in a little water to the mixture.

Place the salmon fillets in a shallow dish and pour half of the teriyaki sauce over them, reserving the other half for later. Marinate the salmon in the sauce for about 15-30 minutes.

While the salmon is marinating, prepare the stir-fried vegetables. Heat vegetable oil in a large skillet or wok over medium-high heat.

- Add minced garlic and grated ginger to the skillet and cook for about 30 seconds until fragrant.
- Add the mixed vegetables to the skillet and stir-fry for 4-5 minutes, or until they are crisp-tender.
- In a small bowl, mix together soy sauce, rice vinegar, and sesame oil. Pour the mixture over the vegetables and toss to coat evenly. Season with salt and pepper to taste. Remove from heat and set aside.
- Preheat your oven to 400°F (200°C). Line a baking sheet with parchment paper or aluminum foil.
- Remove the salmon fillets from the marinade and place them on the prepared baking sheet. Discard any excess marinade.
- Bake the salmon in the preheated oven for 12-15 minutes, or until it flakes easily with a fork and is cooked to your desired level of doneness.
- While the salmon is baking, heat the remaining teriyaki sauce in a small saucepan over medium heat. Bring it to a simmer and let it cook for a few minutes until it thickens slightly.
- Once the salmon is done baking, remove it from the oven and brush it with the thickened teriyaki sauce.
- Serve the Teriyaki Salmon with Stir-Fried Vegetables hot, garnished with sesame seeds and chopped green onions if desired.
- Enjoy your delicious and flavorful meal!

This Teriyaki Salmon with Stir-Fried Vegetables is a healthy and satisfying dish that's perfect for a quick and easy weeknight dinner. The salmon is tender and flavorful, and the stir-fried vegetables add a delicious crunch and freshness to the meal. Feel free to customize the recipe with your favorite vegetables and adjust the seasoning to suit your taste preferences.

Turkey and Veggie Lettuce Wraps

Ingredients:

For the Turkey Filling:

- 1 lb ground turkey
- 1 tablespoon olive oil
- 1 small onion, finely chopped
- 2 cloves garlic, minced
- 1 bell pepper, diced
- 1 zucchini, diced
- 1 carrot, grated
- 1 cup mushrooms, diced
- 1 teaspoon ground cumin
- 1 teaspoon chili powder
- Salt and pepper to taste
- Optional: chopped fresh cilantro or green onions for garnish

For Serving:

- Large lettuce leaves (such as iceberg, romaine, or butter lettuce)
- Optional toppings: diced tomatoes, avocado slices, shredded cheese, salsa, sour cream, hot sauce

Instructions:

Heat olive oil in a large skillet over medium heat. Add the chopped onion and minced garlic and cook for 2-3 minutes until softened and fragrant.

Add the ground turkey to the skillet and cook, breaking it up with a spoon, until it is browned and cooked through, about 5-7 minutes.

Once the turkey is cooked, add the diced bell pepper, diced zucchini, grated carrot, and diced mushrooms to the skillet. Cook for another 5-7 minutes, or until the vegetables are tender.

Stir in the ground cumin, chili powder, salt, and pepper, and cook for another minute to allow the flavors to meld together. Taste and adjust seasoning if needed.

Remove the skillet from heat and let the mixture cool slightly.

To serve, spoon the turkey and veggie mixture onto large lettuce leaves, using them as wraps.
Top the lettuce wraps with optional toppings such as diced tomatoes, avocado slices, shredded cheese, salsa, sour cream, or hot sauce.
Garnish with chopped fresh cilantro or green onions if desired.
Serve the Turkey and Veggie Lettuce Wraps immediately and enjoy!

These lettuce wraps are light, flavorful, and packed with protein and veggies, making them a healthy and satisfying meal option. They're perfect for a quick and easy lunch or dinner, and you can customize them with your favorite toppings and seasonings. Feel free to experiment with different vegetables or add-ins to suit your taste preferences.

Whole Wheat Pasta Primavera

Ingredients:

- 8 oz whole wheat pasta (such as penne or fusilli)
- 2 tablespoons olive oil
- 2 cloves garlic, minced
- 1 onion, thinly sliced
- 1 bell pepper, thinly sliced
- 1 zucchini, thinly sliced
- 1 yellow squash, thinly sliced
- 1 cup cherry tomatoes, halved
- 1 cup broccoli florets
- 1 cup sliced mushrooms
- Salt and pepper to taste
- 1/4 cup grated Parmesan cheese (optional)
- Fresh basil or parsley leaves for garnish (optional)

Instructions:

Cook the whole wheat pasta according to the package instructions until al dente. Drain and set aside, reserving some pasta water.
In a large skillet, heat the olive oil over medium heat. Add the minced garlic and sauté for about 30 seconds, until fragrant.
Add the sliced onion to the skillet and cook for 2-3 minutes until softened.
Add the sliced bell pepper, zucchini, yellow squash, cherry tomatoes, broccoli florets, and sliced mushrooms to the skillet. Cook for 5-7 minutes, stirring occasionally, until the vegetables are tender but still crisp.
Season the vegetables with salt and pepper to taste.
Add the cooked whole wheat pasta to the skillet with the vegetables. Toss everything together gently to combine.
If the pasta seems dry, add a splash of reserved pasta water to loosen it up and create a sauce.
Optional: Sprinkle grated Parmesan cheese over the pasta primavera and toss to combine.
Remove the skillet from heat.
Serve the Whole Wheat Pasta Primavera hot, garnished with fresh basil or parsley leaves if desired.
Enjoy your delicious and nutritious meal!

This Whole Wheat Pasta Primavera is loaded with colorful vegetables and whole grains, making it a healthy and satisfying dish. It's perfect for a quick and easy weeknight dinner, and you can customize it with your favorite vegetables and herbs. Feel free to add grilled chicken or shrimp for extra protein, or swap out the Parmesan cheese for a dairy-free alternative to make it vegan-friendly.

Greek Yogurt Parfait with Mixed Nuts and Honey

Ingredients:

- 1 cup Greek yogurt (plain or vanilla)
- 1/4 cup mixed nuts (such as almonds, walnuts, pecans, or pistachios), chopped
- 2 tablespoons honey
- 1/4 cup granola (optional, for added crunch)
- Fresh berries or sliced fruit for garnish (optional)

Instructions:

In a serving glass or bowl, layer the Greek yogurt, mixed nuts, and honey.
If using granola, add a layer on top of the nuts.
Repeat the layers until the glass or bowl is filled, ending with a drizzle of honey on top.
Optional: Garnish with fresh berries or sliced fruit for added flavor and presentation.
Serve the Greek Yogurt Parfait with Mixed Nuts and Honey immediately and enjoy!

This parfait is a quick and nutritious breakfast or snack option. The Greek yogurt provides protein and probiotics, while the mixed nuts add healthy fats and crunch. The honey adds natural sweetness, and the granola (if using) adds additional texture and fiber. Feel free to customize the parfait with your favorite nuts, fruits, or toppings to suit your taste preferences.

Lentil and Vegetable Curry

Ingredients:

- 1 cup dry lentils (green or brown), rinsed
- 2 tablespoons olive oil
- 1 onion, diced
- 2 cloves garlic, minced
- 1 tablespoon fresh ginger, minced
- 1 bell pepper, diced
- 2 carrots, diced
- 1 zucchini, diced
- 1 cup cauliflower florets
- 1 can (14 oz) diced tomatoes
- 1 can (14 oz) coconut milk
- 2 tablespoons curry powder
- 1 teaspoon ground turmeric
- 1 teaspoon ground cumin
- 1 teaspoon ground coriander
- 1/2 teaspoon chili powder (adjust to taste)
- Salt and pepper to taste
- Fresh cilantro leaves for garnish (optional)
- Cooked rice or naan bread for serving

Instructions:

In a large pot or Dutch oven, heat olive oil over medium heat. Add diced onion and cook until softened, about 3-4 minutes.

Add minced garlic and ginger to the pot and cook for an additional minute until fragrant.

Stir in curry powder, ground turmeric, ground cumin, ground coriander, and chili powder. Cook for another minute to toast the spices.

Add diced bell pepper, carrots, zucchini, and cauliflower florets to the pot. Cook for 5-7 minutes, stirring occasionally, until the vegetables are slightly softened.

Add rinsed lentils, diced tomatoes (with their juices), and coconut milk to the pot. Stir well to combine.

Bring the mixture to a boil, then reduce the heat to low. Cover and simmer for about 20-25 minutes, or until the lentils and vegetables are tender and the curry has thickened.

Season the lentil and vegetable curry with salt and pepper to taste.

Serve the lentil and vegetable curry hot, garnished with fresh cilantro leaves if desired. Serve with cooked rice or naan bread on the side.

Enjoy your delicious Lentil and Vegetable Curry!

This curry is hearty, nutritious, and packed with flavor. The combination of lentils, vegetables, and aromatic spices makes it a satisfying vegetarian meal option. It's perfect for a cozy dinner or meal prep for lunches throughout the week. Feel free to customize the recipe by adding your favorite vegetables or adjusting the spices to suit your taste preferences.

Baked Chicken Thighs with Rosemary and Garlic

Ingredients:

- 4-6 bone-in, skin-on chicken thighs
- 3 cloves garlic, minced
- 2 tablespoons fresh rosemary leaves, chopped
- 2 tablespoons olive oil
- 1 tablespoon lemon juice
- Salt and pepper to taste

Instructions:

Preheat your oven to 400°F (200°C).
In a small bowl, mix together the minced garlic, chopped rosemary leaves, olive oil, lemon juice, salt, and pepper to create a marinade.
Pat the chicken thighs dry with paper towels. This helps the skin crisp up while baking.
Place the chicken thighs in a large bowl or shallow dish. Pour the marinade over the chicken thighs, making sure to coat them evenly. You can also rub the marinade under the skin for extra flavor.
Arrange the chicken thighs, skin-side up, on a baking sheet lined with parchment paper or aluminum foil.
Bake the chicken thighs in the preheated oven for 35-40 minutes, or until the skin is crispy and golden brown, and the internal temperature reaches 165°F (74°C) when measured with a meat thermometer.
Once done, remove the chicken thighs from the oven and let them rest for a few minutes before serving.
Serve the baked chicken thighs hot, garnished with additional fresh rosemary leaves if desired.
Enjoy your delicious Baked Chicken Thighs with Rosemary and Garlic!

These baked chicken thighs are tender, juicy, and packed with flavor from the aromatic rosemary and garlic marinade. They pair well with a variety of side dishes such as roasted vegetables, mashed potatoes, or a fresh salad. Feel free to customize the recipe by adding other herbs or spices to the marinade, or adjusting the cooking time to achieve your desired level of doneness.

Egg White Breakfast Burrito with Salsa

Ingredients:

- 4 large egg whites
- 1 whole wheat tortilla
- 1/4 cup shredded cheese (cheddar, Monterey Jack, or your favorite cheese)
- 1/4 cup salsa (store-bought or homemade)
- Salt and pepper to taste
- Optional toppings: sliced avocado, diced tomatoes, chopped cilantro, sour cream

Instructions:

In a small bowl, whisk together the egg whites until frothy. Season with salt and pepper to taste.
Heat a non-stick skillet over medium heat. Pour the whisked egg whites into the skillet and cook, stirring occasionally, until they are set and cooked through.
Once the egg whites are cooked, remove them from the skillet and set aside.
Warm the whole wheat tortilla in the skillet for a few seconds on each side until it becomes pliable.
Place the cooked egg whites in the center of the tortilla. Sprinkle shredded cheese on top of the egg whites.
Add salsa on top of the cheese.
Optional: Add any additional toppings you like such as sliced avocado, diced tomatoes, chopped cilantro, or sour cream.
Fold the sides of the tortilla over the filling, then roll it up tightly into a burrito.
Place the burrito back in the skillet seam-side down and cook for a minute or two on each side until the tortilla is golden brown and crispy.
Once done, remove the breakfast burrito from the skillet and serve hot.
Enjoy your Egg White Breakfast Burrito with Salsa!

This breakfast burrito is quick, easy, and nutritious, making it a perfect option for busy mornings. The egg whites provide protein, while the salsa adds flavor and a kick of heat. Feel free to customize the recipe by adding your favorite fillings or adjusting the seasonings to suit your taste preferences.

Stuffed Portobello Mushrooms with Quinoa and Spinach

Ingredients:

- 4 large Portobello mushrooms
- 1 cup quinoa, rinsed
- 2 cups vegetable broth or water
- 2 tablespoons olive oil
- 2 cloves garlic, minced
- 4 cups fresh spinach leaves, chopped
- 1/4 cup grated Parmesan cheese
- Salt and pepper to taste
- Optional toppings: chopped fresh herbs (such as parsley or basil), red pepper flakes, additional grated Parmesan cheese

Instructions:

Preheat your oven to 375°F (190°C).

Remove the stems from the Portobello mushrooms and gently scrape out the gills using a spoon. Place the mushrooms on a baking sheet lined with parchment paper or aluminum foil, gill side up.

In a medium saucepan, bring the vegetable broth or water to a boil. Add the rinsed quinoa and reduce the heat to low. Cover and simmer for 15-20 minutes, or until the quinoa is cooked and the liquid is absorbed. Remove from heat and fluff the quinoa with a fork.

In a large skillet, heat the olive oil over medium heat. Add the minced garlic and cook for 1-2 minutes until fragrant.

Add the chopped spinach to the skillet and cook, stirring occasionally, until wilted.

Add the cooked quinoa to the skillet with the spinach and garlic. Stir well to combine.

Remove the skillet from heat and stir in the grated Parmesan cheese. Season with salt and pepper to taste.

Spoon the quinoa and spinach mixture into each of the Portobello mushroom caps, pressing down gently to pack the filling.

Optional: Sprinkle chopped fresh herbs, red pepper flakes, or additional grated Parmesan cheese on top of the stuffed mushrooms for added flavor.

Bake the stuffed Portobello mushrooms in the preheated oven for 20-25 minutes, or until the mushrooms are tender and the filling is heated through.
Once done, remove the stuffed mushrooms from the oven and let them cool slightly before serving.
Serve the Stuffed Portobello Mushrooms with Quinoa and Spinach hot as a delicious and nutritious vegetarian meal.

Enjoy your flavorful and satisfying Stuffed Portobello Mushrooms with Quinoa and Spinach! These mushrooms make a hearty and nutritious main course or a tasty side dish for any occasion. Feel free to customize the recipe by adding your favorite herbs, spices, or additional toppings to suit your taste preferences.

Turkey and Black Bean Chili

Ingredients:

- 1 tablespoon olive oil
- 1 onion, diced
- 2 cloves garlic, minced
- 1 bell pepper, diced
- 1 jalapeño pepper, seeded and diced (optional, for extra heat)
- 1 lb ground turkey
- 1 can (15 oz) black beans, drained and rinsed
- 1 can (14.5 oz) diced tomatoes
- 1 cup chicken or vegetable broth
- 2 tablespoons tomato paste
- 2 teaspoons chili powder
- 1 teaspoon ground cumin
- 1 teaspoon dried oregano
- 1/2 teaspoon paprika
- Salt and pepper to taste
- Optional toppings: shredded cheese, chopped green onions, chopped cilantro, sour cream, avocado slices, lime wedges

Instructions:

Heat the olive oil in a large pot or Dutch oven over medium heat.
Add the diced onion, minced garlic, diced bell pepper, and diced jalapeño pepper (if using) to the pot. Cook, stirring occasionally, until the vegetables are softened, about 5-7 minutes.
Add the ground turkey to the pot. Cook, breaking it up with a spoon, until it is browned and cooked through.
Stir in the drained and rinsed black beans, diced tomatoes, chicken or vegetable broth, tomato paste, chili powder, ground cumin, dried oregano, paprika, salt, and pepper.
Bring the chili to a simmer, then reduce the heat to low. Cover and let it simmer for about 20-25 minutes, stirring occasionally, to allow the flavors to meld together and the chili to thicken.
Taste and adjust the seasoning, adding more salt, pepper, or chili powder if needed.

Once the chili is done cooking, remove it from heat.
Serve the Turkey and Black Bean Chili hot, garnished with your favorite toppings such as shredded cheese, chopped green onions, chopped cilantro, sour cream, avocado slices, or lime wedges.
Enjoy your delicious and hearty Turkey and Black Bean Chili!

This chili is comforting, flavorful, and packed with protein and fiber. It's perfect for a cozy dinner on a cold day, and leftovers can be stored in the refrigerator for a few days or frozen for longer-term storage. Feel free to customize the recipe by adding other vegetables, beans, or spices to suit your taste preferences.

Grilled Vegetable Salad with Chickpeas

Ingredients:

For the Grilled Vegetables:

- 2 bell peppers (red, yellow, or orange), sliced into strips
- 1 zucchini, sliced lengthwise into strips
- 1 yellow squash, sliced lengthwise into strips
- 1 eggplant, sliced into rounds
- 1 red onion, sliced into rounds
- 2 tablespoons olive oil
- Salt and pepper to taste

For the Salad:

- 1 can (15 oz) chickpeas (garbanzo beans), drained and rinsed
- 4 cups mixed salad greens (such as lettuce, spinach, arugula)
- 1/4 cup fresh basil leaves, torn
- 1/4 cup fresh parsley leaves, chopped
- 1/4 cup crumbled feta cheese (optional)
- 2 tablespoons balsamic vinegar
- 2 tablespoons extra virgin olive oil
- Salt and pepper to taste

Instructions:

Preheat your grill to medium-high heat.
In a large bowl, toss the sliced bell peppers, zucchini, yellow squash, eggplant, and red onion with olive oil, salt, and pepper until evenly coated.
Grill the vegetables on the preheated grill until they are tender and slightly charred, about 5-7 minutes per side. Remove from the grill and let them cool slightly.
In a large salad bowl, combine the grilled vegetables, chickpeas, mixed salad greens, torn basil leaves, and chopped parsley.
If using, sprinkle crumbled feta cheese over the salad.

In a small bowl, whisk together the balsamic vinegar and extra virgin olive oil to make the dressing. Season with salt and pepper to taste.

Drizzle the dressing over the salad and toss gently to combine, ensuring that all ingredients are coated evenly.

Taste and adjust seasoning if needed.

Serve the Grilled Vegetable Salad with Chickpeas immediately as a delicious and nutritious meal.

Enjoy your flavorful and satisfying salad!

This Grilled Vegetable Salad with Chickpeas is packed with flavor, fiber, and nutrients. It's perfect for a light lunch or dinner, and you can customize it with your favorite vegetables and toppings. Feel free to add grilled chicken, tofu, or shrimp for extra protein, or swap out the feta cheese for a vegan-friendly alternative.

Tofu and Vegetable Stir-Fry with Brown Rice

Ingredients:

For the Tofu:

- 14 oz block extra-firm tofu
- 2 tablespoons soy sauce
- 1 tablespoon sesame oil
- 1 tablespoon cornstarch
- 1 tablespoon vegetable oil, for frying

For the Stir-Fry Sauce:

- 1/4 cup soy sauce
- 2 tablespoons hoisin sauce
- 1 tablespoon rice vinegar
- 1 tablespoon sesame oil
- 1 tablespoon brown sugar
- 2 cloves garlic, minced
- 1 teaspoon grated ginger
- 1 tablespoon cornstarch
- 1/4 cup water

For the Stir-Fry:

- 2 tablespoons vegetable oil
- 1 onion, sliced
- 2 bell peppers, sliced
- 2 cups broccoli florets
- 1 cup sliced carrots
- 2 cups cooked brown rice

Instructions:

Press the tofu: Wrap the block of tofu in a clean kitchen towel and place it on a plate. Put a heavy object, such as a cast-iron skillet or a couple of cans, on top of the tofu and let it press for about 30 minutes to remove excess moisture.
Cut the pressed tofu into cubes and place them in a bowl. In a separate small bowl, mix together 2 tablespoons soy sauce, 1 tablespoon sesame oil, and 1

tablespoon cornstarch. Pour this marinade over the tofu cubes and gently toss to coat. Let the tofu marinate for about 15-20 minutes.

In a small bowl, whisk together all the ingredients for the stir-fry sauce: 1/4 cup soy sauce, hoisin sauce, rice vinegar, sesame oil, brown sugar, minced garlic, grated ginger, 1 tablespoon cornstarch, and 1/4 cup water. Set aside.

Heat 1 tablespoon of vegetable oil in a large skillet or wok over medium-high heat. Add the marinated tofu cubes and cook until golden brown on all sides, about 5-7 minutes. Remove the tofu from the skillet and set aside.

In the same skillet, add 2 tablespoons of vegetable oil. Add the sliced onion, bell peppers, broccoli florets, and sliced carrots. Stir-fry the vegetables for about 5-7 minutes, or until they are tender-crisp.

Return the cooked tofu to the skillet with the vegetables.

Pour the prepared stir-fry sauce over the tofu and vegetables in the skillet. Cook, stirring constantly, until the sauce thickens and coats the tofu and vegetables, about 2-3 minutes.

Serve the tofu and vegetable stir-fry hot over cooked brown rice.

Enjoy your delicious Tofu and Vegetable Stir-Fry with Brown Rice!

This tofu and vegetable stir-fry is packed with flavor, protein, and nutrients. It's a healthy and satisfying meal that's perfect for a quick and easy weeknight dinner. Feel free to customize the recipe by using your favorite vegetables or adding additional spices and seasonings to suit your taste preferences.

Baked Cod with Mango Salsa

Ingredients:

For the Baked Cod:

- 4 cod fillets (about 6 ounces each)
- 2 tablespoons olive oil
- 1 teaspoon paprika
- 1 teaspoon garlic powder
- 1 teaspoon dried thyme
- Salt and pepper to taste
- Lemon wedges for serving

For the Mango Salsa:

- 1 ripe mango, peeled, pitted, and diced
- 1/2 red bell pepper, diced
- 1/4 cup red onion, finely chopped
- 1 jalapeño pepper, seeded and finely chopped
- 1/4 cup fresh cilantro, chopped
- Juice of 1 lime
- Salt and pepper to taste

Instructions:

Preheat your oven to 400°F (200°C). Line a baking sheet with parchment paper or aluminum foil.

Place the cod fillets on the prepared baking sheet. Drizzle olive oil over the fillets and sprinkle with paprika, garlic powder, dried thyme, salt, and pepper, ensuring they are evenly coated.

Bake the cod in the preheated oven for 12-15 minutes, or until the fish is opaque and flakes easily with a fork.

While the cod is baking, prepare the mango salsa. In a medium bowl, combine the diced mango, red bell pepper, red onion, jalapeño pepper, cilantro, and lime juice. Season with salt and pepper to taste. Mix well to combine.

Once the cod is done baking, remove it from the oven and transfer it to serving plates.

Spoon the mango salsa over the baked cod fillets.

Serve the Baked Cod with Mango Salsa immediately, garnished with additional cilantro and lemon wedges on the side.
Enjoy your flavorful and nutritious meal!

This Baked Cod with Mango Salsa is light, fresh, and bursting with tropical flavors. The combination of tender baked cod and sweet and tangy mango salsa creates a perfect balance of flavors and textures. It's a quick and easy dish to prepare for a healthy weeknight dinner or a special occasion. Feel free to customize the salsa with additional ingredients such as diced avocado, cherry tomatoes, or pineapple for extra freshness and flavor.

Turkey and Quinoa Stuffed Zucchini

Ingredients:

- 4 medium zucchinis
- 1 tablespoon olive oil
- 1 onion, diced
- 2 cloves garlic, minced
- 1 bell pepper, diced
- 1 lb ground turkey
- 1 cup cooked quinoa
- 1 teaspoon dried oregano
- 1 teaspoon dried basil
- Salt and pepper to taste
- 1/2 cup shredded mozzarella cheese (optional)
- Fresh parsley for garnish (optional)

Instructions:

Preheat your oven to 375°F (190°C). Grease a baking dish with cooking spray or olive oil.

Cut the zucchinis in half lengthwise. Use a spoon to scoop out the flesh from the center, leaving about a 1/4-inch border around the edges. Reserve the flesh for later use.

Heat olive oil in a large skillet over medium heat. Add diced onion and cook until softened, about 3-4 minutes.

Add minced garlic and diced bell pepper to the skillet. Cook for another 2-3 minutes until fragrant.

Add ground turkey to the skillet and cook until browned, breaking it up with a spoon as it cooks.

Chop the reserved zucchini flesh and add it to the skillet. Cook for an additional 3-4 minutes until the zucchini is tender.

Stir in cooked quinoa, dried oregano, dried basil, salt, and pepper. Cook for another 2-3 minutes to allow the flavors to meld together. Taste and adjust seasoning if needed.

Spoon the turkey and quinoa mixture into the hollowed-out zucchini halves, pressing down gently to pack the filling.

Place the stuffed zucchini halves in the prepared baking dish. If desired, sprinkle shredded mozzarella cheese over the top of each stuffed zucchini.

Cover the baking dish with aluminum foil and bake in the preheated oven for 25-30 minutes, or until the zucchini is tender and the filling is heated through. Once done, remove the foil and broil for an additional 2-3 minutes until the cheese is melted and bubbly.

Garnish the Turkey and Quinoa Stuffed Zucchini with fresh parsley before serving, if desired.

Serve hot and enjoy your delicious and nutritious meal!

This Turkey and Quinoa Stuffed Zucchini is a healthy and satisfying dish that's perfect for a light dinner or lunch. It's packed with protein, fiber, and flavor, making it a crowd-pleaser for the whole family. Feel free to customize the recipe with your favorite herbs, spices, or additional toppings to suit your taste preferences.

Greek Yogurt Ranch Dip with Veggies

Ingredients:

For the Greek Yogurt Ranch Dip:

- 1 cup Greek yogurt (plain or flavored)
- 1 tablespoon ranch seasoning mix (store-bought or homemade)
- 1 tablespoon lemon juice
- 1 tablespoon chopped fresh dill (optional)
- Salt and pepper to taste

For the Veggie Platter:

- Assorted fresh vegetables, such as carrot sticks, cucumber slices, bell pepper strips, celery sticks, cherry tomatoes, broccoli florets, and snap peas

Instructions:

In a small bowl, mix together the Greek yogurt, ranch seasoning mix, lemon juice, and chopped fresh dill until well combined.
Taste the dip and season with salt and pepper as needed.
Transfer the Greek Yogurt Ranch Dip to a serving bowl and garnish with additional chopped dill, if desired.
Arrange the assorted fresh vegetables on a platter or serving tray around the bowl of dip.
Serve the Greek Yogurt Ranch Dip with Veggies immediately and enjoy!

This dip is creamy, flavorful, and packed with protein from the Greek yogurt. It pairs perfectly with a variety of fresh vegetables, making it a healthy and delicious snack or appetizer option for parties, gatherings, or everyday snacking. Feel free to customize the dip by adding your favorite herbs or spices, or adjusting the consistency with a splash of milk or water if desired.

Chicken Caesar Salad with Whole Wheat Croutons

Ingredients:

For the Salad:

- 2 boneless, skinless chicken breasts
- 1 tablespoon olive oil
- Salt and pepper to taste
- 1 head romaine lettuce, washed and chopped
- 1/4 cup grated Parmesan cheese
- Whole wheat croutons (see recipe below)
- Caesar salad dressing (store-bought or homemade)

For the Whole Wheat Croutons:

- 2 cups whole wheat bread, cut into cubes
- 2 tablespoons olive oil
- 1/2 teaspoon garlic powder
- 1/2 teaspoon dried basil
- 1/2 teaspoon dried oregano
- Salt and pepper to taste

Instructions:

Preheat your oven to 375°F (190°C).
Season the chicken breasts with salt and pepper. In a skillet over medium-high heat, heat 1 tablespoon of olive oil. Add the chicken breasts and cook for about 6-8 minutes on each side, or until cooked through and no longer pink in the center. Remove from heat and let the chicken rest for a few minutes. Once rested, slice the chicken into thin strips.
While the chicken is cooking, prepare the whole wheat croutons. In a large bowl, toss the whole wheat bread cubes with olive oil, garlic powder, dried basil, dried oregano, salt, and pepper until evenly coated. Spread the bread cubes in a single layer on a baking sheet. Bake in the preheated oven for 10-12 minutes, or until the croutons are golden brown and crispy. Remove from the oven and let them cool.

In a large salad bowl, combine the chopped romaine lettuce, grated Parmesan cheese, sliced chicken breast strips, and whole wheat croutons.

Drizzle Caesar salad dressing over the salad, starting with a small amount and adding more as desired. Toss the salad gently to coat everything evenly with the dressing.

Serve the Chicken Caesar Salad with Whole Wheat Croutons immediately and enjoy!

This Chicken Caesar Salad with Whole Wheat Croutons is a classic and satisfying meal that's perfect for lunch or dinner. The whole wheat croutons add a delicious crunch and extra fiber to the salad, while the homemade Caesar dressing brings all the flavors together. Feel free to customize the salad with additional toppings such as cherry tomatoes, sliced cucumbers, or avocado slices, and adjust the dressing to suit your taste preferences.

Black Bean and Sweet Potato Enchiladas

Ingredients:

For the Enchilada Filling:

- 2 medium sweet potatoes, peeled and diced
- 1 can (15 oz) black beans, drained and rinsed
- 1 small onion, diced
- 2 cloves garlic, minced
- 1 teaspoon ground cumin
- 1 teaspoon chili powder
- 1/2 teaspoon paprika
- Salt and pepper to taste
- 2 tablespoons olive oil

For the Enchilada Sauce:

- 2 tablespoons olive oil
- 2 tablespoons all-purpose flour
- 2 tablespoons chili powder
- 1 teaspoon ground cumin
- 1/2 teaspoon garlic powder
- 1/4 teaspoon dried oregano
- 2 cups vegetable broth
- Salt to taste

For the Enchiladas:

- 8-10 corn tortillas
- 1 cup shredded cheese (cheddar, Monterey Jack, or your favorite cheese)
- Chopped fresh cilantro for garnish (optional)
- Sour cream or Greek yogurt for serving (optional)
- Sliced avocado for serving (optional)

Instructions:

Preheat your oven to 375°F (190°C). Grease a 9x13-inch baking dish with cooking spray or olive oil.

In a large skillet, heat 2 tablespoons of olive oil over medium heat. Add diced sweet potatoes and cook for 5-7 minutes, or until they begin to soften.

Add diced onion and minced garlic to the skillet with the sweet potatoes. Cook for another 2-3 minutes until the onions are translucent and fragrant.

Stir in drained and rinsed black beans, ground cumin, chili powder, paprika, salt, and pepper. Cook for an additional 2-3 minutes to heat through and combine the flavors. Remove from heat and set aside.

To make the enchilada sauce, heat 2 tablespoons of olive oil in a saucepan over medium heat. Whisk in all-purpose flour, chili powder, ground cumin, garlic powder, and dried oregano. Cook for 1-2 minutes, stirring constantly, until the mixture is fragrant and lightly golden.

Gradually whisk in vegetable broth, stirring constantly to prevent lumps from forming. Cook the sauce for 5-7 minutes, or until it thickens to your desired consistency. Season with salt to taste. Remove from heat and set aside.

To assemble the enchiladas, warm the corn tortillas slightly to make them pliable. You can do this by wrapping them in a damp paper towel and microwaving for 30-60 seconds, or by heating them briefly in a dry skillet.

Spoon a portion of the sweet potato and black bean filling onto each tortilla, then roll them up tightly and place seam-side down in the prepared baking dish.

Pour the enchilada sauce evenly over the rolled-up tortillas in the baking dish. Sprinkle shredded cheese over the top.

Cover the baking dish with aluminum foil and bake in the preheated oven for 20-25 minutes, or until the enchiladas are heated through and the cheese is melted and bubbly.

Once done, remove the foil and bake for an additional 5 minutes to lightly brown the cheese.

Remove the enchiladas from the oven and let them cool for a few minutes before serving.

Garnish with chopped fresh cilantro, and serve with sour cream or Greek yogurt and sliced avocado on the side, if desired.

Enjoy your delicious Black Bean and Sweet Potato Enchiladas!

These enchiladas are flavorful, hearty, and satisfying, perfect for a vegetarian dinner option or for anyone looking for a meatless meal. Feel free to customize the recipe by adding your favorite toppings such as salsa, diced tomatoes, or sliced jalapeños.

Protein-Packed Green Smoothie with Kale and Pineapple

Ingredients:

- 1 cup unsweetened almond milk (or your choice of milk)
- 1 scoop vanilla protein powder (whey, plant-based, or your preferred type)
- 1 cup fresh kale leaves, stems removed
- 1 cup frozen pineapple chunks
- 1/2 ripe banana
- 1 tablespoon chia seeds or flaxseeds
- Optional: honey or maple syrup to taste for added sweetness
- Ice cubes (optional, if you prefer a colder smoothie)

Instructions:

Add the unsweetened almond milk to the blender.
Add the vanilla protein powder to the blender.
Add the fresh kale leaves to the blender.
Add the frozen pineapple chunks to the blender.
Add the ripe banana to the blender.
Add the chia seeds or flaxseeds to the blender.
If desired, add honey or maple syrup to the blender for added sweetness.
Optional: Add ice cubes to the blender if you prefer a colder smoothie.
Blend all the ingredients until smooth and creamy. If needed, stop the blender and scrape down the sides with a spatula to ensure all ingredients are well incorporated.
Once the smoothie reaches your desired consistency, pour it into a glass and enjoy immediately.
Optionally, you can garnish the smoothie with additional pineapple chunks or a sprig of fresh mint for presentation.
Enjoy your protein-packed green smoothie with kale and pineapple as a nutritious and delicious breakfast or snack!

This smoothie is not only delicious but also packed with nutrients from the kale, pineapple, and protein powder. It's a great way to start your day on a healthy note or refuel after a workout. Feel free to customize the recipe by adding other ingredients such as spinach, mango, or avocado to suit your taste preferences.

www.ingramcontent.com/pod-product-compliance
Lightning Source LLC
LaVergne TN
LVHW081610060526
838201LV00054B/2188